Queen Iween's

To Be a Honey Bee, Like Me!

Irene T. Hunt, Author and Photographer
Timothy J. Hunt, Editor and Photographer

HƒN

Hunt for Nature Publishing
San Diego, California

www.HuntForNature.com

Special thanks to

Tim Hunt, an amazing husband and photographer!

My family and friends for their love, encouragement and support!

The most amazing Bee Lady, Diane Busch, and her father, Joe Deavenport, for loving, nurturing and protecting so many precious little honey bees!

George L. Jones and Everett E. Whitbeck, Sr. for their many years of devotion to honey bees!

Mark and Priscilla Whitbeck for contributing their beautiful photographs!

My educational consultant, Susan Walker, for her valuable insights!

My illustrator, Nate Robb, for his incredible creativity!

***

Are you looking for other Queen Iween books? Visit www.HuntForNature.com.

Library of Congress Control Number: 2010913849
Summary: Queen Iween entertains and educates children with facts about her honey bee family.
ISBN #978-0-9843071-2-8
[1. Children 2. Honey Bees 3. Pollination 4. Photography]
First Edition: September 2010   10 9 8 7 6 5 4 3 2 1

Hᵖ⫀N
Hunt for Nature Publishing
San Diego, California

For information about Hunt for Nature Publishing visit our website at
www.HuntForNature.com
or send an email to QueenIween@HuntForNature.com.

Queen Iween books are made in the U.S.A.

Queen Iween's
To Be a Honey Bee, Like Me!

If you were a honey bee, like me, you would:

This book is dedicated to all those devoted beekeepers who strive to ensure the health and well being of honey bees for many generations to come.

Work, work, work
That's the life of a honey bee
It's all about the health of the colony
We go from flower to flower as you will see
Gathering food for the family

Work, work, work
That's the life of a honey bee
We may get close when there's activity
It's just your movement that we see
If you leave us be, you'll be sting free
That's the life of a honey bee

Work, work, work
That's what is important to me

4

Hello my friend!

My name is Queen Iween and I am a honey bee. We are very special creatures.

Would you like to learn about honey bees? Are you ready?

Come see what it would be like if you were a honey bee, like me.

5

If you were a honey bee, like me...

You might live in a small space like a box, or a log, or in a big place like a tree. Your home could be anywhere if you built it securely.

Your house would be a beehive full of honeycomb rooms with wax walls. Every honeycomb room, called a cell, would be filled with honey, pollen, or a baby honey bee. We honey bees keep a very neat and clean house. We work day and night doing our household chores.

Are you neat and clean, like a honey bee?

Beehives are full of wax honeycomb that the honey bees fill with either honey, pollen, or baby honey bees.

If you were a honey bee, like me...

Your hive would be full of family living together in a colony.

Your beehive could be home to more than 20,000 members of your family, and maybe as many as 100,000. That is a lot of honey bees living together. When some creatures, like honey bees, ants, bats and beavers, live and grow together, the group is called a "colony". In your beehive colony you would have sisters, brothers, and your mother, the queen bee, living with you.

How many people do you live with?
How are you related?

A honey bee family lives together in a colony. There could be as many as 100,000 brother and sister honey bees in the colony. **9**

If you were a honey bee, like me...

Your brothers would be few and your sisters plenty.

You would have a lot more sisters than brothers. Girl bees do more work for the colony than boys, so the queen bee lays more girl eggs. She needs all the help she can get. Your brother bees would be called "drones" and your sisters would be called "worker bees". That is how it is in the honey bee world.

Do you have brothers and sisters? How many?

Boy honey bees, called drones, are bigger than their sisters and have much bigger eyes. Can you see the boy honey bee in the middle, surrounded by all his worker bee sisters?

If you were a honey bee, like me...

You would be so busy you would be called a busy little bee.

CHORES To Be Done

Your sisters would be called "worker bees" because they work all the time, both inside and outside of the hive. Worker bees have chores to do and they do them day and night. Their chores change as they get older. Your younger worker bee sisters would be called "house bees", because they start with chores inside the hive, like cleaning the honeycomb cells. Then they begin taking care of their mother, the queen, and all of her baby bees. When they are old enough to make wax they will begin building honeycomb cells, and guarding the door to the hive. Finally, when they are old enough, they become "field bees". Field bees spend all day long outside gathering food and water for the colony.

What chores do you do at home? Which is your favorite chore?

A worker bee and her sister doing their chores. They collect pollen, nectar, and water for the colony.

If you were a honey bee, like me...
Your mother would be the one and only Queen bee.

Each hive has only ONE queen bee! She is longer than all the other bees and is the only girl bee that can lay eggs. She can lay as many as 2,000 eggs each day. A queen bee only leaves the hive once or twice in her life because she is so busy laying eggs. The bigger her family the more workers she will have to gather food and water. Without food and water the colony cannot survive, and neither can you!

What other animals lay eggs?

The longest bee in the hive is the queen bee. Can you see the queen bee with all of her daughters around her? Her daughters are called worker bees. They take care of their mother, the queen. **15**

If you were a honey bee, like me...

You would know the secret to being a queen is royal jelly.

Royal jelly is not like the jelly you put on a peanut butter and jelly sandwich. It is much more special than that. Royal jelly is made by house bees for the queen bee. A queen is a member of a royal family, that is why the jelly is called "royal jelly". Baby bees are fed a little royal jelly and lots of bee bread, a mixture of pollen and nectar. Queen bee babies are only fed the richest food, royal jelly. The royal jelly makes a baby bee become a queen bee. It's so rich in nutrients that it makes her bigger than all the other bees, and it gives her the ability to lay eggs.

What foods do you eat that help you grow to be big and strong?

ROYAL JELLY

The queen bee lays her eggs in the honeycomb cells and the worker bees feed them a little royal jelly, and lots of bee bread. Then the worker bees put wax caps on the cells to help the larvae develop into honey bees. Can you see the honey bee larvae curled up in the cells?

If you were a honey bee, like me...
You would belong to the insect family.

Insects have two antennae, six legs, and three body parts: a head, thorax, and abdomen. Insects also have a hard outer covering on their body, called an exoskeleton. In order to grow, they have to shed their exoskeleton, just like caterpillars.

Butterflies and ladybugs are insects too. What other insects do you like?

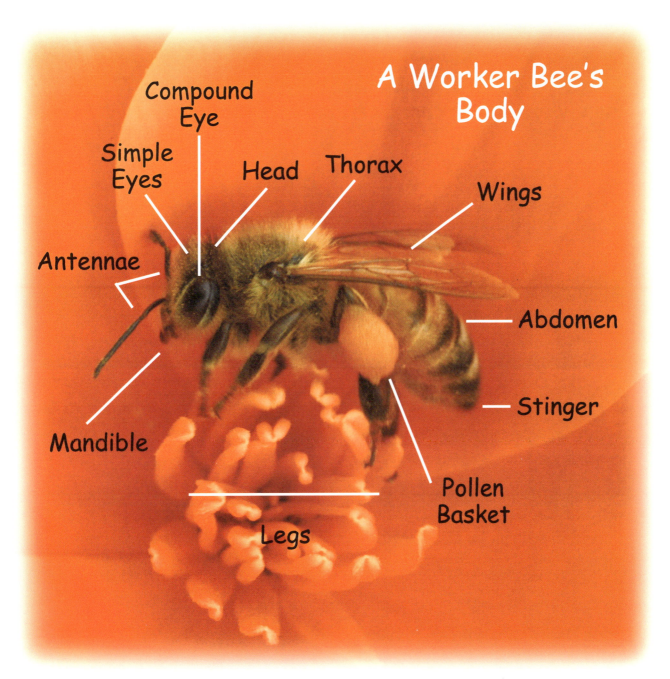

A Worker Bee's Body

Compound Eye

Simple Eyes

Head

Thorax

Wings

Antennae

Abdomen

Mandible

Stinger

Pollen Basket

Legs

The honey bee is a member of the insect family. Can you close your eyes and name all the body parts of a honey bee?

If you were a honey bee, like me...

In the dark your antennae would help you move around freely without the need for eyes to see.

As a honey bee you would have two antennae on the top of your head. Your antennae would help you find your way around the dark hive. That is because antennae are like your nose and fingers. They help honey bees to smell and feel their way around. You would also use your antennae to find your favorite food, the sweet nectar that hides in flowers.

What would it be like to have your nose and fingers on the top of your head?

With the use of its antennae, a honey bee searches for nectar in a bird of paradise flower. Antennae also help guide honey bees in the dark.

If you were a honey bee, like me...

The color red you would not see, it would
be as black as the screen on a turned-off TV.

The color red would
look black. Yes, black! Honey
bees cannot see the color red, but
they can see green, yellow, and blue.
They can also see colors that you can't,
which are called ultraviolet colors.

Honey bees have more eyes than you. We
have two big compound eyes and three simple
eyes. That's five eyes. Our compound eyes let
us see color, movement, and shapes, and our
simple eyes detect the amount of light.
Compound eyes are big and easy to see on the
sides of our head, but our simple eyes are
very small. Simple eyes are located on the
tip top of our head and they form
a triangle.

What do you think the world
would look like if you could
see through five eyes?

Simple
Eyes

Compound
Eyes

Can you see the honey bee's five eyes? There are two big
compound eyes and three little simple eyes. The simple eyes
form a triangle on the top of the honey bee's head.

23

If you were a honey bee, like me...

Your legs would come in two pairs of three, and funny enough, they would be hairy.

You would have six hairy legs, three on each side of your abdomen. When worker bees walk across flowers, pollen gets stuck in the hairs on their legs and body. When they are ready to fly, they move the pollen into the pollen baskets on their two back legs. The pollen baskets hold the pollen and nectar so that it can be carried back to the hive by the worker bee. Drones don't have pollen baskets because boys don't gather pollen and nectar for the hive. Only worker bees have pollen baskets.

What do you use to carry your food when you are shopping at the grocery store?

Worker bees have a special place on their back legs to put pollen and nectar. They are called pollen baskets, and they help the worker bees to carry the pollen and nectar back to the hive. **25**

If you were a honey bee, like me...

A stinger you would have only if you were a girl bee.

Not all honey bees have a stinger like me, the queen bee. Worker bees have stingers because their job is to protect the hive, and collect food and water for the colony. Drones don't do those things, so they do not have a stinger. If you've ever been stung by a honey bee, then you were stung by a girl bee. Worker bees cannot live without their stingers, so they only sting when they need to protect themselves or their colony. Queen bees can use their stingers over and over again, but they don't leave the hive very often so it's unlikely you would ever get stung by a queen bee.

What kind of honey bee would you like to be?

The worker bee is showing you where her stinger is located.

Her stinger is at the very tip of her abdomen. Only girl bees, like worker bees and queen bees, have stingers.

A worker bee's stinger is very, very small. This is a close up picture of a stinger.

Worker bees can only sting one time because they lose part of their abdomen when they sting. They can't live without their abdomen.

If you were a honey bee, like me...

You would use your proboscis when you were hungry.

FLOWER JUICE

You would have a long straw-like tongue, called a proboscis (pro-bahs-kis). You would use your proboscis to suck nectar from flowers. It's like using a straw in a juice box. You would also have two sets of jaws, called mandibles (man-di-buls). You could use your mandibles for many things like chewing on wax to soften it for the honeycombs, or you could use it to bite a flower so it will release pollen.

Do you like to use a straw when you drink?

Did you know that your lower jaw is also called a mandible?

Is this worker bee sticking her tongue out at you? No, she is just getting ready to use her proboscis to sip nectar from the flower. It is best not to bother her when she is eating and working.   **29**

If you were a honey bee, like me...

You could dance a little dance for all
the honey bees to see.

Honey bees communicate with each other by dancing. When worker bees find food close by they return to the hive and perform their "round" dance. They go round and round, first in one direction and then the other. The dance tells the other bees that pollen and nectar are close by. When food is farther away they do the "waggle" dance. They waggle their bodies as they make a figure 8. They do this many times. How fast they dance and how loud they buzz lets the other worker bees know where to go to find food.

Can you do one of the honey bee dances? Which dance is more fun?

With her proboscis hanging out, a worker bee heads for a flower full of nectar. She will then fly back to her hive to do her dance, telling all her sisters where to go to find the flowers she visited. **31**

If you were a honey bee, like me...

Your kitchen would be the flowers you visit so frequently.

A flower would be your kitchen, because that's where you would go to find food to eat. We need flowers and flowers need us. Flowers make nectar so that we, and other insects and animals, will stop by for a visit. While we feed on the flower's nectar, the pollen sticks to our bodies, and we carry it to many other flowers we visit. That helps flowers to make seeds, which then grow into new plants. This is called pollination (pa-lehn-a-shun). Bees are not the only ones that help to pollinate flowers and plants.

Can you name other insects and animals that help pollinate flowers and plants?

Pollen sticks to the hairs on a honey bee's body. As the honey bee visits other flowers, pollen falls off of her body and pollinates the flowers.

If you were a honey bee, like me...
You could make the sweetest of sweets, called honey.

Honey is thick, sticky, and as sweet as candy. It's yummy on your toast and in your oatmeal. Honey bees make honey from nectar that worker bees collect from flowers. They store the honey in the honeycomb. In the winter when it's cold, and there are no more flowers, we eat the honey and pollen that is stored in the honeycombs. That is how we survive until spring when the weather gets warmer and the flowers begin to bloom again.

Do you like honey? What yummy things do you eat with honey?

A worker bee tries to get a last little sip of honey from the honeycomb before the beekeeper takes it away. Beekeepers only take what they need, leaving more than enough for the colony to eat.

If you were a honey bee, like me...

You would pollinate flowers and plants accidentally, helping them to produce foods that are very tasty.

You would be very special! Everyone who loves food and drinks such as: lemonade, orange juice, apple juice, peach cobbler, peanut butter, blueberry muffins, apple pie and watermelon, should love honey bees. Why is that? That's because we help pollinate all the plants that are used to make these yummy-in-your-tummy goodies. Everyone would be sad if we were not here to help make pretty flowers, healthy foods, and yummy sweets.

What's your favorite food or juice that honey bees help to make? Can you think of more?

A honey bee pollinates the flower of a mandarin orange tree.

Once the flowers are pollinated, baby mandarin oranges will begin to grow.

Oranges are green when they are babies, but they turn orange as they ripen and are ready to eat.

How many baby oranges can you see?

Queen Iween's Quiz

1. What do honey bees put in their **honeycomb cells?** (Page 6)

2. What is a girl honey bee called? (Page 10)

3. Are there more worker bees in a beehive, or **drones**? (Page 10)

4. Which honey bee is the longest bee in the hive? (Page 14)

5. What is **royal jelly** used for? (Page 16)

6. How many legs does a honey bee have? (Page 18)

7. Which color looks black to a honey bee? (Page 22)

8. How does a worker bee carry **pollen** back to the **beehive?** (Page 24)

9. Which honey bees have **stingers**? (Page 26)

10. What does a honey bee do with its **proboscis**? (Page 28)

11. What do honey bees eat? (Pages 28 and 34)

12. Why do **honey bees** dance? (Page 30)

13. How do honey bees help plants? (Page 32)

14. What is **honey** made from? (Page 34)

15. How are honey bees able to survive in the winter when all the flowers are gone? (Page 34)

I have some secrets I want to share with you. They will help you and my worker bees too.

They are the SECRETS to staying sting free! I bet you dislike getting stung just as much as worker bees dislike stinging you. Since I'm helping you by sharing my secrets, will you help me?

SECRETS

1. Never throw anything at bees or their beehive!

2. Honey bees don't like honey-loving bears, so don't look like a bear!
   a. Bears are dark colored and hairy, so wear light-colored clothes, and a hat when you play near flowers.
   b. Bears are very STINKY! Don't be stinky too.

3. Wear peppermint oil! Bees will avoid you if you smell like peppermint.

4. Do not eat bananas before you play near flowers, the smell will attract bees.

5. Never swat at a honey bee, just back away.

5 Great Ideas For How You Can Help Honey Bees!

Great Idea #1
Let your garden grow wild!

Honey bees love wildflowers, especially those that are yellow, blue, or purple. Dandelions, sunflowers, and poppies are some of their favorite wildflowers.

Learn about the wildflowers that are native to your area, so that you can plant flowers that will grow easily.

Great Idea #2
Plant fruit trees, vegetables and herbs!

If you provide food for the honey bees, they will help provide food for you.

Fruit trees and vegetable plants will give the honey bees plenty of food, and the bees will help pollinate your plants. Some of their favorite trees and plants are: orange, lemon, apple, pear, avocado, cherry, raspberry, grape, watermelon, cucumber, carrot, broccoli, and strawberry.

Honey bees also love flowering herbs, like basil, chives, lavender, rosemary, thyme, sage, and mint. Let your herbs flower so the honey bees can enjoy their nectar and pollen.

Great Idea #3
Help keep your yard safe for honey bees!

Ask your family not to use chemicals in your yard. Chemicals hurt honey bees and honey bee friendly flowers and plants. There are natural ways of controlling pests in your yard.

Being nice to bees is helpful too. If you see them, just leave them alone. Honey bees will come back to your garden if they feel safe. If honey bees build a hive in a place you do not like, call a beekeeper. The beekeeper may be able to take the bees and their hive to a better place.

Great Idea #4
Help your local Beekeepers!

Ask your family to buy honey from your local beekeeper. It's better for you and they need your support!

Great Idea #5
Help spread the word!

Share what you have learned with everyone you know so they will be honey bee friendly just like you!

It was so fun to share
my family with you. I hope you
had fun too.

Don't forget that we honey bees are very
important because we help to produce food
for everyone and everything in the world.

If you see one of us don't be scared,
"Just bee calm and you'll bee fine,
the only thing honey bees
want to do is dine."

Glossary

Abdomen (ab-duh-men)

The rear body part of an insect.

Antenna (an-ten-uh)

One of a pair of long, thin body parts on the head of insects, crabs, and other animals. Depending on the animal, antenna are used to feel, smell, or taste.

Bee Bread (bee bred)

A mixture of pollen and nectar that worker bees feed to honey bee babies while they are in the honeycomb cells.

Beehive (bee-hive)

A nest for bees, usually above the ground.

Colony (kahl-o-nee)

A group of the same species of creatures that live and grow together, like honey bees, ants, bats, and beavers. Not all animals live in a colony, some live in herds, flocks, troops, etc.

Drone (droan)

A male bee that has no stinger and does not gather nectar and pollen.

Exoskeleton (ek-soh-skel-eh-tehn)

A hard outer structure that provides protection or support for an animal.

Honey (hun-ee)

A thick, sticky, sugary food made by honey bees from the nectar of flowers. They store it in honeycombs for them to eat.

Honey Bee (hun-ee bee)

A bee that makes honey and lives in a colony.

Honeycomb (hun-ee-coam)

Six-sided wax cells grouped together, and built by honey bees in their hive.

Honeycomb Cell (hun-ee-coam sell)

A six-sided wax room that honey bees use to store their honey and pollen. They also grow their babies in the cells.

Larva (lar-vuh)

An insect after it hatches from an egg and before it changes into an adult. It has no wings and looks like a worm.

Glossary - Page 2

Mandible (man-di-bul)

The first pair of mouthparts of some invertebrates and arthropods that is often used for biting.

Pollen (pa-lehn)

The fine powder-like material made by flowering plants that helps the plant make new plants.

Pollination (pa-lehn-a-shun)

The process of moving or carrying pollen from one plant or flower to another.

Proboscis (pro-bahs-kis)

The slender, tubular, feeding and sucking structure of certain invertebrates, such as insects.

Queen Bee (kween bee)

The fully developed female of social bees whose purpose is to lay eggs.

Royal Jelly (roy-al jel-lee)

A substance rich in nutrients that comes from glands in the head of honey bees. It is fed to all baby bees but more is given to queen bees.

Stinger (sting-er)

A sharp organ of some animals, like bees, that is used for protection.

Thorax (tho-rax)

The middle part of an insect's body that is located between the head and abdomen.

Ultraviolet Color (ultra-vio-let)

A color that people cannot see, but is visible by some birds and insects.

Worker Bee (wurk-er bee)

A female member of a honey bee colony that does most of the work and protects the colony.

We would love to hear your thoughts on our books. Our email addresses are:
Irene@HuntForNature.com
Tim@HuntForNature.com.

For a listing of Queen Iween books please visit our website,
www.HuntForNature.com.

LaVergne, TN USA
20 October 2010

201502LV00001BA